W9-BMZ-398

If found, please return to: _____

_____

_____

_____

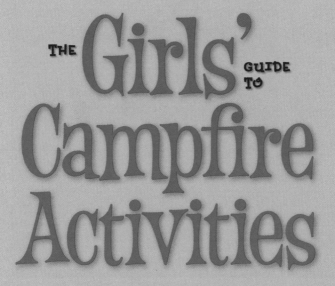

THE Girls' GUIDE TO Campfire Activities

THE Girls' GUIDE TO Campfire Activities

- Great for Sleepovers!!
- Safely Build a Wood Fire
- Make Awesome S'mores
- Tell Chilling Ghost Stories
- Host a Campfire Slumber Party

By Elizabeth Encarnacion

APPLESAUCE PRESS

Kennebunkport, Maine

Fires can be dangerous and even deadly. Kids should always be supervised by an adult when working with fire and should follow all of the instructions and safety rules in this book, as well as any local fire regulations.

13-Digit ISBN: 978-1-60433-003-8
10-Digit ISBN: 1-60433-003-1

This book may be ordered by mail from the publisher. Please include $2.50 for postage and handling.
Please support your local bookseller first!

Books published by Applesauce Press and Cider Mill Press Book Publishers are available at special discounts for bulk purchases in the United States by corporations, institutions, and other organizations. For more information, please contact the publisher.

Cider Mill Press Book Publishers
"Where good books are ready for press"
12 Port Farm Road
Kennebunkport, Maine 04046

Visit us on the Web!
www.cidermillpress.com

Designed by Ponderosa Pine Design, Vicky Vaughn Shea
Illustrations by Lisa Perrett
Photography by: Ron Chapple/Getty Images, ©iStock.com/Reynir Hauksson, ©JupiterImages
www.thinkstock.com, ©iStock.com/Nancy Louie

Printed in China

1 2 3 4 5 6 7 8 9 0
First Edition

Contents

Introduction

✳ ✳ ✳

The crisp smell of burning wood, and the warmth of a crackling fire. The gooey sweetness of s'mores, and the thrill of a creepy ghost story. The silly songs that make you laugh, and the ones about friendship that make you cry. The best campfires pack all of this and more into one amazing night, giving you memories that will last a lifetime.

Whether your idea of camping is backpacking the Appalachian Trail or crashing on sleeping bags in your living room, you can plan the perfect campfire that's sure to impress and delight your friends. Just make sure you cover the three Fs: fire, food, and fun! If you're camping, you may be able to host a classic bonfire for roasting marshmallows and telling tales. Indoors, you'll need to use your creativity to set the proper mood and find good substitutes for the fire, food, and fun!

CHAPTER 1

Everything You Need to Know about Building a Fire

The best campfires involve more than just sitting around a roaring fire, but the fire's still the main event. For a traditional campfire, you'll want to build a wood fire in a fire circle, with wooden logs or other seats placed around it. In a pinch (such as in a thunderstorm), you can build a charcoal fire in a fireplace under a shelter or cook marshmallows over a propane camp stove.

When building a wood fire, it helps to think of it as a wild animal. Just like all animals, including humans, it needs shelter, air, heat, and food in order to survive. The shelter is a fire circle, which keeps the fire safely contained in one place and also helps block strong gusts of wind. The fire also needs air, so the fire structure should be packed with just a few small sticks at first so that the fire can breathe. The heat comes from the match that you use to light it. And the food is the wood that you slowly add to the fire to help it grow larger.

Being Smart about Safety

Like a wild animal, fire can hurt you, especially when it gets out of control or you don't treat it with respect. You should always have an adult help you when you're working with fire, just in case something goes wrong. If your parents or guardians aren't sure that they want you to learn how to build a fire, talk to them about it and show them the note for adults on the next page. Tell them that you'd like to learn the safe way to make a fire with their help.

When building a fire, treat it with respect at all times and follow all of the safety guidelines. If you do get hurt, refer to the first aid instructions for burns or see a doctor.

A Note for Adults:
Why Kids Should Learn about Fire

A significant percentage of accidental fires are started by children playing with matches. Kids and teens who have learned the safe way to start a fire under your supervision will be less curious about fire and will not feel the need to experiment with it. Through the process of building the fire and putting it out, they will also learn respect for the fire, and will understand how it spreads and how to contain it. This knowledge will take away much of the mystery and excitement that makes kids want to play with matches in the first place.

Choosing a Spot

The first step in building your campfire is to choose the perfect spot. Many campsites have a permanent fire circle for this purpose, with seats made from logs or stumps arranged in a circle around it. Make sure the fire circle is in good condition and replace any missing rocks in the circle. Clear out any leaves or sticks that have fallen into the circle.

Remove pieces of charred wood and piles of ashes left from earlier campfires. Large pieces of partially burned wood can be used in your fire once it is going strong, but should not be used to start it. Rake the area so that you have a clear, flat surface on which to build your fire.

Checking Fire Regulations

Before you arrive at your campsite, you should check with the local fire department or forestry office to make sure open-air fires are allowed. They may also have rules about the type of fire that you can build or the weather conditions when you can build a fire. Even campsites that usually allow fires may forbid them during a drought or strong winds.

Making a Fire Circle

If your campsite doesn't have a fire circle, you'll have to build one yourself.

1. Find a flat, dirt-covered area away from low overhanging trees, roots, dry grasses, tents, or other things that could catch on fire.
2. Clear out any leaves, sticks, grass, or rocks from the area until you have formed a circle that is about six feet in diameter.
3. Place large rocks (or, in a pinch, large green logs) near the edge of the clearing to form a fire circle. Do not use rocks from a riverbed, as they could explode. The rocks will help keep sparks safely inside the fire circle and provide some protection from the wind.
4. Around the outer edge of the clearing, place large logs or tree stumps for seating.

Gathering Wood

Before you start to build the fire, you'll need to gather enough wood to start the fire and keep it going for several hours. Look for fallen branches that snap or break when bent but are not rotten. Branches that bend without breaking, look green inside, or are cut fresh off a tree have not dried out and will not burn.

You'll need to collect three basic types of fire-building material to start your fire and keep it going.

Tinder

Tinder is natural material that will burn immediately when touched by a flame. Finding good tinder is the most important part of gathering wood, since the tinder is what keeps the fire going for the first few minutes until the larger sticks catch fire. Without tinder, you'll end up with a lot of used matches and no flame.

Tinder must be small, thin, and very dry. Wood shavings, dried leaves, dried pine needles, or dead bark all make good tinder. If your campsite doesn't have a lot of tinder nearby, you can also use twisted paper, dryer lint, sawdust, or used matches. You should gather several handfuls of tinder for your woodpile.

Kindling

Twigs that are small enough to catch fire quickly, but large enough to burn longer than tinder are called kindling. Kindling is used to build the fire's strength until it can set fire to larger pieces of wood. Pieces of kindling are usually thicker than a match but thinner than your thumb. Be sure to collect kindling in many different sizes so that you can build the fire gradually. Collect enough kindling to fill a bucket.

Fuel

Fuel is the name for larger pieces of wood that feed the fire and keep it burning. Any stick or log that is thicker than your thumb is considered fuel. You'll need to gather a wide range of fuel in different sizes to build and maintain your fire. Thinner sticks can be carefully broken into foot-long pieces, but larger branches may need to be sawed into logs with an adult's help. Gather enough fuel in different sizes to form a good-sized woodpile.

Some campsites, especially those at state parks and wilderness areas, do not allow you to gather fallen wood. Check the rules at your campsite, and buy or bring wood with you if necessary.

Making a Woodpile

Once you've collected plenty of firewood, you'll want to stack it into a neat woodpile before you start your fire. Your woodpile should be outside the seating area around your fire circle, but not too far away. To build a base that will keep your wood dry, lay a few thick branches horizontally on the ground and stack your wood across them. Start with the tinder on one side, followed by the kindling, placed from thinnest to thickest, then the fuel also arranged by size. If your firewood keeps mixing together, leave a little space between the different sizes of wood or use branches stuck into the ground to keep them separate.

It's very important to keep your woodpile dry, so be sure to cover it with a plastic tarp at night when dew forms and during rainstorms. Stake the edges down with sticks or use rocks to weigh down the corners. If some of your fuel gets wet, try stacking a few pieces near the fire to dry out.

The Fire Bucket

When building a wood fire, you should always have a large fire bucket filled with water sitting on the edge of the fire circle. Check to make sure it is full every time before laying your fire. A shovel is also useful for covering an out-of-control fire with dirt.

The Girls' Guide to Campfire Activities

Choosing the Best Kind of Fire

So, you've checked the local fire regulations, collected a beautiful pile of firewood, and filled your fire bucket with water. Before you can lay your fire and light it, you'll need to choose the best shape for your purposes.

- Are you a fire-building beginner? Do you want a simple fire that's easy to make and good for most purposes? Are you roasting marshmallows or cooking hot dogs? Build an A-Frame fire.
- Are you building a fire that will be used to cook with pots and pans or a grill? Build a Log Cabin fire.
- Are you hoping for a campfire with big flames? Making a bonfire for a camp-wide gathering? Want a fire that can be seen from far away? Build a Teepee fire.
- Are you building a fire in wet or windy conditions? Build a Lean-To fire.

Now that you know which kind of fire you want to build, it's time to learn how to lay a fire.

Laying a Wood Fire

Laying a fire simply means getting the firewood ready to be lit with a match. Each type of fire requires a structure built from several pieces of thick kindling and a handful of tinder placed in the center of the structure. However, as you might guess, each one has its own special shape inspired by the structure it was named after.

A-Frame Fire

Choose three thick pieces of kindling about the thickness of your thumb. With the wind to your back, make a letter A. The crossbar of the A should lie on top of the two sides of the letter to allow air underneath.

Have two handfuls of tinder, a large pile of kindling, and some small pieces of fuel at hand. Place a handful of the tinder inside the A, leaning against the crossbar. Lean two or three thin pieces of kindling on the crossbar, over the tinder.

Log Cabin Fire

This one is very similar to the A-Frame fire, except with four sides instead of only three. Place a handful of tinder

A-Frame Fire

Log Cabin Fire

Teepee Fire

Lean-To Fire

in the center of the fire circle. Lay two pieces of thick kindling around the tinder, one on each side. Stack two more thick pieces of kindling on top of the first two to form a square, overlapping the ends. Continue to alternate directions and add kindling until the tinder is well protected.

Teepee Fire

Place a handful of tinder in the center of the fire circle. Carefully stand three pieces of kindling on their ends and lean them against each other, over the tinder. (If possible, use a stick with a forked end for one of the pieces to help stabilize the other two.) Gently lean additional pieces of kindling against the structure, leaving some open spaces for air.

Lean-To Fire

Set a small log in the fire circle and place a handful of tinder alongside it. Put pieces of kindling over the tinder, leaning on the log.

Good Enough to Eat

If you're a first-time fire-builder, practice your skills with food. It's a yummy way to stay safe and test yourself, and it makes a great snack!

YOU'LL NEED:

- A napkin
- Mini marshmallows
- A cup of juice
- Pretzel logs
- Coconut shavings
- Thin pretzel sticks
- Small red candies

1. Spread your napkin on the table as your cleared area. Build a fire circle with mini marshmallows.
2. Set your fire bucket filled with juice next to the fire circle.
3. Use three pretzel logs to form an A-frame.
4. Put a pile of tinder made from coconut shavings in the circle, leaning against the crossbar of the A.
5. Lean a few pieces of pretzel stick kindling over the tinder.

6. Use a pretzel stick to "light" the tinder. Practice placing additional kindling on the fire as it grows stronger.

7. Sprinkle a few red candies on the fire to represent flames. Begin carefully adding larger pretzel logs to build the fire.

8. Eat the fire foods as your successful fire begins to die down.

Get Ready, Get Set...

When starting your fire, follow these safety rules:

- ✪ Pull your hair back with a ponytail holder or a headband.
- ✪ Wear long pants to protect your legs from burns.
- ✪ Do not wear clothing with hanging strings, cords, tassels, or anything else that might catch fire.
- ✪ Always strike the match away from your body, and discard used matches in a safe place away from flammable material.

Starting a Fire

Once your tinder and kindling is laid out in the fire circle and ready to go, it's time to get this fire started. You'll definitely need to ask an adult to help out—even adults who are starting a fire should have another person around to help in case of an emergency.

Before you pull out the matches, check your fire bucket one more time to make sure it is full of water and sitting by your fire circle. You should also have an extra handful of tinder, a small handful of kindling in different sizes, and a handful of small fuel within reach. Now, let's get started.

1. Squat down just outside the fire circle. Carefully strike a match and wait until it catches. Hold the flame under the tinder in your A-frame or other structure until the tinder catches fire.

2. Place a bit more tinder on the fire. Start leaning the smallest pieces of kindling over the tinder, leaving some space between sticks.

3. If the tinder stops flaming before the kindling catches on fire, gently blow on the smoking tinder to give it more air. Add more tinder if necessary. Be sure to look away between breaths so you don't inhale smoke.

4. As the kindling catches fire, continue layering slightly larger pieces of kindling over the fire, one at a time. Slowly build the fire, using slightly thicker sticks as the previous ones catch on fire.

5. When the kindling is burning strong, begin to add small pieces of fuel to make the shape you want. As you are building the fire, always add sticks or logs that are less than twice as big as the last piece of fuel you added. The thicker the log, the longer it will take to catch on fire.

How to Strike a Match

If you've never used matches before, you may want to practice lighting a few before trying to start a campfire.

Be sure to ask an adult for help whenever you're using matches. Blow out the match before the flame burns down near your finger. Dunk used matches in water to make sure they're out before you throw them away.

1. Hold the match between your thumb and pointer finger.
2. Hold the matchbox in your other hand, with the striking surface facing you.
3. Slide the tip of the match along the striking surface, moving away from you. Push firmly, but not hard enough to snap the match in half.
4. If the match lights, hold it away from the matchbox and your clothes. If it does not, rotate the tip of the match and try again.
5. If the matches are lighting briefly and then going out, try cupping your hand around the flame to protect it from drafts.
6. To put the flame out, blow a puff of air at the tip of the match. Dunk the match in water.

Around the Fire

Once the fire is burning, follow these rules to stay safe:

- Never run near the fire.
- Always walk around the fire circle. Never step across or inside the circle.
- Keep flammable objects away from the fire.
- Don't place anything too close to the fire, especially shoes (which can melt), roasting sticks (which can catch fire), or food (which can get ashes on it).
- When tending the fire, never throw wood into the fire. Always place it carefully, one piece at a time.

Bad Weather

It's challenging, but not impossible, to build a campfire in the wind or rain. Just remember to give your fire a shelter to protect it from these elements and you should be fine.

Starting a Fire in Wind

If the wind is too strong, it may not be safe to build a fire because the wind could blow sparks out of the fire circle and cause a wildfire. If the breeze is safe but still causing fire-building problems, place a large rock or log inside the fire circle between the wind and your fire to help block the gusts. You could also ask a couple of friends to squat outside of the fire circle on the windy side while you're getting the fire going.

If you still can't get the tinder and kindling to flame, try using a homemade egg-carton fire starter, which will burn longer and stronger than tinder. Using a Lean-To fire set-up will provide some protection for the fire while it's just getting started and keep burning tinder from flying away. Once you get your fire going, keep an eye out for flying sparks.

Starting a Fire in Rain

When it rains, you'll need to tackle the problem from three angles. First, you should keep your matches in a waterproof container at all times—even when there isn't a cloud in the sky. Putting your matchbox inside a sealed plastic bag works perfectly. Secondly, you'll need to keep your woodpile covered with a waterproof tarp during storms. Finally, in heavier rain, you may want to build your fire under some kind of shelter, whether it's tall, leafy trees or a nonflammable tarp.

If the fire circle surface is too wet, try building a platform for your fire out of flat stones or several green logs. You can also use a homemade waterproof fire starter called a trench candle that will burn long enough to dry out the kindling and get your fire going.

Fire Starters

The best fire starters are the pieces of tinder that you find in nature, like dried pine needles, leaves, and small twigs. However, in certain conditions, you might need a little extra help. Here are instructions for making two homemade fire starters with common household ingredients.

Egg-Carton Fire Starters

YOU'LL NEED:

- Dryer lint
- A cardboard egg carton
- Paraffin

1. Collect a bunch of lint from your clothes dryer filter. (Sawdust also works well.)
2. Fill each cardboard egg section half full with the lint.
3. With an adult's help, melt paraffin or pieces of candle wax in a double boiler. Carefully pour the melted wax into each egg section until it is full.
4. Allow the fire starters to cool completely.
5. To use, break one egg section off and place it amongst the tinder. Light the edges of the cardboard and layer kindling over top to build the fire as usual.

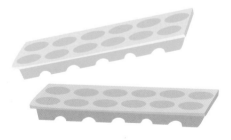

Trench Candles

YOU'LL NEED:

- Newspaper
- String
- Scissors
- Paraffin

1. Separate several sheets of newspaper and roll them into a long, tight roll.
2. Tie string around the roll in several places, leaving one end of each string long (at least 9 inches). The strings should be tied about 3 inches apart.
3. Cut the newspaper roll between the strings for make several shorter pieces.
4. With an adult's help, melt paraffin or pieces of candle wax in a double boiler.
5. Holding the long ends of the strings, carefully dip each piece of newspaper roll into the wax, covering it completely.
6. Hang the fire starters by the strings and allow to dry completely.
7. To use, cut the long string off. Place the trench candle amongst the tinder. Light with a match and layer kindling over top to build the fire as usual.

Fire Tending

Now that your fire is burning bright, you'll need to continue building it into the right shape for your purposes. If you want a simple campfire for cooking s'mores and singing songs, add fuel to the fire steadily until it burns down into red-hot coals. This will give you a satisfying fire with plenty of flames that will slowly transform into an intense bed of coals for roasting marshmallows. Later, as you add fuel only occasionally, the fire will die down and give your ghost stories the perfect spooky atmosphere.

Coals are actually hotter than flames, and burn longer and at a more even temperature. Therefore, they are perfect for cooking in foil packets or stewing food for a longer time in a pot. Again, feed the fire with plenty of fuel in the beginning, and then once the wood has become

coals, nestle your food down into the embers to cook. If necessary, you can put your food on one side of the fire and add fuel to the other side to create more hot coals. Then carefully move your food to the new embers.

If you need to boil water fast, add your fuel in a teepee or cone shape. This focuses all the heat into one spot, instead of spreading it out.

Regardless of how you are growing your fire, you'll want to follow a few basic rules:

1. Wood is a precious natural resource. Use as little as possible to get the result you want. (In other words, don't build a monster bonfire that will last till morning to roast a few marshmallows.)

2. When tending a fire, move in slow motion. Each piece of fuel should be carefully placed into the fire, not tossed or dropped.

3. Never poke or stir the fire while it's burning. That could send sparks flying or burning logs rolling out of the fire circle.

4. Do not pick up burning wood.

5. Any piece of wood added to the fire should fit completely within the fire circle.

First Aid for Burns

Even if you're being careful, it's easy to accidentally burn yourself when you're working with fire. If you do get burned, follow these steps:

1. Get away from the fire or whatever burned you.

2. Check to see how bad the burn is. If it breaks the skin, blisters, turns brown, black, or white, or covers a large portion of skin, call an emergency number immediately.

3. Run cold, clean water over the burn to cool it down. Do not use ice or ice water, as it can cause further damage.

4. Place a sterile bandage over the burn. Do not put anything else on the wound (including first aid creams, ointments, or petroleum jelly).

Putting the Fire Out

Embers can burn for a long time after a fire's flames have died out. You'll need to patiently put the fire out by sprinkling water on the coals until they are completely cool. Follow these steps and you'll have a safe end to your special night.

1. As you near the end of your campfire, stop adding fuel to the fire and allow the wood that is already there to burn as completely as possible.

2. Once the fire has died down and only coals are left, carefully use a long stick to separate pockets of glowing embers and to break apart soft pieces of charcoal.

3. Sprinkle a handful of water over the ashes. The ashes will probably sizzle as the water hits the hot coals, so watch out for hot steam and jumping sparks.

4. Stir the ashes gently with a long stick to mix the water in and expose more hot ash.

5. Repeat steps 3 and 4 until the ashes no longer sizzle when water is sprinkled on them, paying special attention to hot spots.

6. Hold your hand several inches above the ashes to check for heat. Repeat steps 3 and 4 in any warm areas.

7. Continue sprinkling and stirring the ashes until you can lower your hand to the surfaces of the ashes without feeling any warmth. At this point, the fire is out.

8. Carry the ashes away from your campsite and spread them over a wide area so that they blend into the dirt. Some campsites may have their own instructions for disposing of ashes.

9. If you built your own fire circle, take it apart and spread the rocks and logs around the campsite where you found them. Spread soil over the fire circle and cover it with the materials that you cleared from it earlier.

CHAPTER 2

I've Got a Fire, Now What Do I Do With It?

How do you put the *camp* in a campfire? Add a little food and fun! After all, a crackling wood fire is certainly warm and inviting, but it's not all that exciting by itself. It needs some tasty treats and girl bonding to make it a can't-miss occasion.

It may not sound like fun, but the key to planning the perfect campfire is just that—planning. Decide what kinds of food you're cooking on the fire—a one-pot meal, a hot dog roast, or a simple dessert? If you're purely in it for the marshmallows, set your campfire to start just as the sun is going down for the full effect. Or, if you're making dinner over the coals, begin a little earlier to give the fire time to burn and turn into embers. Regardless of when you start, choose an end time for the festivities so that you'll know how long to feed the fire.

Next, plan some fun activities to do around the campfire. Save the ghostly tales for when the fire starts to die down, and start off with the goofiest songs you can think of to get everyone giggling. End the night with a few quieter songs that remind you of how much fun you had.

Campfire Cooking

Put your campfire to work by using it to make a snack, dessert, or even your dinner! Stick roasting and foil packet cooking are the easiest (and fastest) ways to cook with a wood fire. S'mores are hugely popular, but if you're camping for more than one day, try one of the other desserts another night. You might find a new favorite!

Roasting on a Stick

There's something special about the taste of a juicy hot dog slowly browned over a campfire, or perfectly toasted marshmallows with gooey goodness oozing out of the center. Roasting food over a bed of hot coals is a great way to cook it quickly and easily—simply slide it onto your roasting stick and hold it over the fire until it browns.

To make a roasting stick, find a fallen branch at least 3 feet long that is still green inside. With an adult's help, peel the bark off one end of the branch. (A pocketknife takes the bark off easily, but should be used with care.) Removing the bark exposes the damp, green part of the branch, which will not catch on fire as easily and is cleaner. Once you've crafted your roasting stick, put it to good use with these recipes.

Delicious Dogs

Hot dogs taste amazing when they're roasted over a hot fire. Toast the buns briefly in the fire to add a little crunch. These have so much flavor that you might decide to skip the ketchup!

YOU'LL NEED:

- Hot dogs
- Aluminum foil
- Hot dog buns

1. Push your roasting stick into one end of the hot dog and through the length of the dog until it almost reaches the other end.

2. Open the bun flat and wrap it in aluminum foil. Set it aside.

3. Roast your hot dog over hot coals, not open flame. Don't get it too close to the coals because ashes could get blown onto your dog. Rotate the stick to lightly brown all sides of the hot dog.

4. When the hot dog is almost ready, place the foil-wrapped bun on coals. The coals will toast the bread very quickly, so use tongs to remove your foil package after just a minute or so.

5. Allow the foil to cool a little and carefully unwrap the bun. Put your hot dog in it and enjoy!

Marvelous Marshmallows

Roasting marshmallows may seem easy, but most people end up turning their marshmallows into a burning torch that eventually falls off the stick and into the fire. Wouldn't you rather get that sticky sweetness into your mouth? Follow these tips to get yours just right. Makes 2 toasted marshmallows.

YOU'LL NEED:

- ⚬ 2 marshmallows

1. Push your roasting stick through the flat end of two marshmallows, one after another. This will help keep them from rolling on the stick as easily.

2. Roast your marshmallows about 4 feet above hot coals. If they begin to brown too quickly, raise them higher or move to embers that aren't as hot. You want them to get a light tan, not a sunburn!

3. Check to make sure your marshmallows are slowly turning a light brown and getting slightly soft inside and a little crunchy outside. If they aren't cooking, move them just a little closer to the coals.

4. Rotate the stick gently to brown all sides of the marshmallows. Once they are lightly brown all around, use them in s'mores or allow them to cool slightly before eating them.

5. If your marshmallows catch on fire, immediately blow them out. You'll want to eat them as soon as they cool off enough, or they'll probably plop onto the ground.

I've Got a Fire, Now What Do I Do With It?

Super Gooey S'mores

S'mores are the ultimate combination of sweet flavors—packed with melted marshmallow, rich chocolate goodness, and crunchy graham crackers. These delightful desserts have been around for a long time—since at least 1927, when the first s'mores recipe appeared in a Girl Scout handbook.

S'mores are super-easy to make—simply take a roasted marshmallow and squeeze it between chocolate and graham crackers. However, to make your s'mores really stand out, use plenty of chocolate and marshmallow for each graham cracker and melt the chocolate a bit first. Makes 6 s'mores.

YOU'LL NEED:

- 6 graham crackers
- 3 milk chocolate bars, such as Hershey's
- Aluminum foil
- 12 marshmallows

1. Carefully break each graham cracker in half to make two squares.
2. Break each chocolate bar in half to make two squares.

Place each chocolate square on a graham cracker half, until six of the graham pieces are covered.

3. Place a piece of aluminum foil on a flat rock in the fire circle, near the coals. Line the chocolate-covered graham cracker squares on the foil so that the heat from the coals slowly starts to melt the chocolate.

4. Roast two marshmallows over coals until they are evenly browned on the outside and gooey on the inside.

5. With the marshmallows still on the roasting stick, place them on a chocolate-covered graham cracker square. Place a plain graham cracker square on top and squeeze, gently pulling the roasting stick out and squishing the marshmallow and chocolate between the two graham crackers.

6. Enjoy the oozing goodness and have s'more!

Amazing Aluminum Foil

Who needs pots and pans when you can cook an entire meal in aluminum foil? Foil packets keep the moisture in and the ashes out, allowing food to cook directly in the coals where the heat is intense. Best of all, each packet holds only one portion, so if you don't like one of the ingredients you can skip it.

When cooking in the coals, make sure to use heavy-duty aluminum foil, which won't rip apart and dump your dinner as easily as regular foil. Some people believe that you should put the shiny side on the inside of the packet to keep the heat in, but it probably doesn't make a big difference.

Inside-Out Apple Crisp

Do you love warm apple crisp fresh out of the oven? Then try this simple foil-wrapped dessert, which takes many of the same ingredients but puts them inside the apple to caramelize as it cooks. Makes 6 apples.

YOU'LL NEED:

- 6 apples
- Aluminum foil
- 1 stick of butter
- Sugar
- Cinnamon

1. Using an apple corer, remove the core from each apple. If you do not have an apple corer, get an adult to help you cut the cores out with a knife.
2. Place each apple on a piece of foil large enough to completely cover the apple.
3. Stuff the center of each apple with about a tablespoon of butter.
4. Sprinkle 2 teaspoons of sugar into each core, along with $1/8$ teaspoon of cinnamon.

5. Wrap the foil securely around each apple. Nestle the apples into hot coals and bake for about 30 minutes, or until the apple is soft throughout.
6. Using tongs and an oven mitt, carefully remove the apples from the fire and set aside to cool off slightly.
7. Once the foil is cool enough to be handled, remove it and enjoy your baked apples.

Baked Banana Boats

If you love banana splits and s'mores, you'll flip for this campfire classic. Melted marshmallow and chocolate mix together inside a gooey baked banana shell, giving this delightful dessert real appeal. Makes 6 banana boats.

YOU'LL NEED:

- 6 bananas
- 1 bag of milk chocolate chips
- 1 bag of mini marshmallows
- Aluminum foil

1. Hold each banana so its ends are pointing up. With an adult's help, use a knife to cut a long wedge out of the length of the banana (cutting through the skin and the flesh). Remove the wedge with the skin still attached.
2. Fill the pocket of each banana with a handful of chocolate chips and a handful of mini marshmallows.
3. Put the banana wedges back in place to hold the filling inside. Tightly wrap the bananas in foil.
4. Nestle the bananas into hot coals and bake for about 20 minutes, or until the chocolate and marshmallows have melted.
5. Using tongs and an oven mitt, carefully remove the bananas from the fire and set aside to cool off slightly.
6. Once the foil is cool enough to be handled, remove it and carefully lift the banana wedge. Use a spoon to eat the banana mixture out of the skin.

Music to My Ears

Songs are an essential part of a successful campfire. Singing humorous songs early in the evening helps loosen everyone up and work off some of their energy. Switch to slower songs later in the night to get people ready for bed and bring extra meaning to the gathering.

When you're sharing a new song with a group, sing it through once so that they can hear how it goes. Then, sing each line and have the group repeat it. If they seem to be learning it, slowly sing it all the way through together. Some of these songs are follow-the-leader songs, where the group is already repeating what the leader sings. For these, simply explain how the song goes and sing the first verse as an example. Then, start over and sing the whole thing through.

Super Silly Songs

Why do people love to sing silly songs at campfires? Maybe it's because it's easier to be goofy when you think no one can see you. Or, perhaps it's in anticipation of that s'mores sugar rush. Whatever the reason, we've given you a few favorites to get you and your friends started on the road to giggles galore.

The Bear Song

Follow-the-leader songs like this one are perfect for campfires because it doesn't matter if part of the group doesn't know the words. Have a few people lead the song, with everyone else repeating the lines. On the last line of each verse, when the verse is being repeated without breaks, the whole group sings together.

The other day, (repeat)
I met a bear, (repeat)
Out in the woods, (repeat)
A-way up there. (repeat)
The other day I met a bear, out in the
    woods, a-way up there.

He looked at me, (repeat)
I looked at him. (repeat)
He sized up me, (repeat)
I sized up him. (repeat)
He looked at me, I looked at him. He sized up
    me, I sized up him.

He said to me, (repeat)
"Why don't you run? (repeat)
I see you ain't (repeat)
Got any gun!" (repeat)
He said to me, "Why don't you run? I see you
    ain't got any gun!"

And so I ran (repeat)
Away from there, (repeat)
But right behind (repeat)
Me was that bear. (repeat)
And so I ran away from there. But right
    behind me was that bear.

Ahead of me, (repeat)
There was a tree, (repeat)
A great big tree, (repeat)
Oh Glory be! (repeat)
Ahead of me, there was a tree, a great big
    tree, oh glory be!

The nearest branch (repeat)
Was ten feet up. (repeat)
I had to jump (repeat)
and trust my luck. (repeat)
The nearest branch was ten feet up. I had to
jump and trust my luck.

And so I jumped (repeat)
Into the air. (repeat)
But I missed that branch, (repeat)
A-way up there. (repeat)
And so I jumped into the air. But I missed
that branch, a-way up there.

Now don't you fret, (repeat)
And don't you frown, (repeat)
'Cause I caught that branch (repeat)
On the way back down! (repeat)
Now don't you fret, and don't you frown,
'cause I caught that branch on the way
back down!

This is the end, (repeat)
There ain't no more, (repeat)
Unless I meet (repeat)
That bear once more! (repeat)
This is the end, there ain't no more, unless I
    meet that bear once more!

And so I met (repeat)
That bear once more. (repeat)
Now he's a rug (repeat)
On my bedroom floor! (repeat)
And so I met that bear once more. Now he's
    a rug on my bedroom floor.

Boom Chicka-Boom

This is a fun follow-the-leader song where each verse has the same words sung in different "accents." Pick a song leader (or two) to chant each line, with everyone else repeating it. Be creative and make up your own "accents" for extra verses.

I said a boom chicka-boom! (repeat)
I said a boom chicka-boom! (repeat)
I said a boom chicka-rocka-chicka-rocka-chicka-boom (repeat)
Uh-huh! (repeat)
Oh, yeah! (repeat)
One more time, (repeat)
[Insert name of next verse] (repeat)

2. Underwater style (sing while dribbling your fingers across your lips)
3. Astronaut style (substitute "I said a zoom chicka-zoom!" and "I said a zoom take a rocket, take a rocket, to the moon!" for the first three lines.)

The Girls' Guide to Campfire Activities

64

4. Baby Style (sing with your thumb in your mouth)
5. Janitor Style (substitute "I said a broom sweepa-broom!" and "I said a broom sweepa-moppa-sweepa-moppa-sweepa-broom!" for the first three lines.)
6. Whisper Style (whisper as softly as you can)
7. Loudmouth Style (yell as loud as you can)

An Austrian Went Yodeling

Test your memory with this song that adds a new sound
effect and hand motion in each verse, while you're
slapping, clapping, and snapping to keep time with this
music. Be creative and add more interruptions with funny
sound effects to make this song longer.

Oh, an Austrian went yodeling
On a mountain so high,
When along came a cuckoo bird,
Interrupting his cry.

Ho—li—ah—
Ho-li-ah ki-ki-ah, ho-li-ah cuc-koo
Ho-li-ah ki-ki-ah, ho-li-ah cuc-koo
Ho-li-ah ki-ki-ah, ho-li-ah cuc-koo
Ho-li-ah, ki-ki-ah, ho.

Oh, an Austrian went yodeling
On a mountain so high,
When along came an avalanche,
Interrupting his cry.

Ho—li—ah—
Ho-li-ah ki-ki-ah, ho-li-ah cuc-koo, swish
Ho-li-ah ki-ki-ah, ho-li-ah cuc-koo, swish
Ho-li-ah ki-ki-ah, ho-li-ah cuc-koo, swish
Ho-li-ah, ki-ki-ah, ho.

Oh, an Austrian went yodeling
On a mountain so high,
When along came a grizzly bear,
Interrupting his cry.

Ho—li—ah—
Ho-li-ah ki-ki-ah, ho-li-ah cuc-koo, swish, grr
Ho-li-ah ki-ki-ah, ho-li-ah cuc-koo, swish, grr
Ho-li-ah ki-ki-ah, ho-li-ah cuc-koo, swish, grr
Ho-li-ah, ki-ki-ah, ho.

Oh, an Austrian went yodeling
On a mountain so high,
When along came a St. Bernard,
Interrupting his cry.

Ho—li—ah—

Ho-li-ah ki-ki-ah, ho-li-ah cuc-koo, swish,
    grr, pant pant

Ho-li-ah ki-ki-ah, ho-li-ah cuc-koo, swish,
    grr, pant pant

Ho-li-ah ki-ki-ah, ho-li-ah cuc-koo, swish,
    grr, pant pant

Ho-li-ah, ki-ki-ah, ho.

Hand motions:

As you sing, slap your thighs, then clap your
hands, then snap your fingers in time to
the music.

On the slow "Ho—li—ah—" at the beginning of
each chorus, slap your thighs to make a
drum roll.

On "swish," make a swishing movement with
your hand.

On "grr," curl your hands like bear claws.

On "pant pant," pant like a dog with your
tongue hanging out.

The Ants Go Marching

Many favorite campfire songs put new, sillier words to a classic tune with a more serious origin. "The Ants Go Marching" is one of these, sung to the tune of the Civil War song "When Johnny Comes Marching Home Again."

The ants go marching one by one, hurrah, hurrah!
The ants go marching one by one, hurrah, hurrah!
The ants go marching one by one,
The last one stopped to suck his thumb

As they all go marching down, to the ground,
   to get out of the rain.

The ants go marching two by two, hurrah,
   hurrah!
The ants go marching two by two, hurrah,
   hurrah!
The ants go marching two by two,
The last one stopped to tie her shoe
As they all go marching down, to the ground,
   to get out of the rain.

Extra verses:
3. three by three...to climb a tree.
4. four by four...to close the door.
5. five by five...to stay alive.
6. six by six...to pick up sticks.
7. seven by seven...to go to heaven.
8. eight by eight...to shut the gate.
9. nine by nine...to check the time.
10. ten by ten...to start again.

Slower Songs

These quiet songs will help bring down the energy level and make you feel close to your friends. We love these three because they're all about campfires and not wanting this magical night to end.

Campfire's Burning

Sung to the tune of the classic British round "London Burning," this version can also be performed as a round. Divide your singers into four groups and give each group a number from one to four. The first group starts singing, and when they get to the second line of the song, the second group starts singing from the beginning, and so on. Repeat the song four times until the fourth group finishes the last line alone.

Campfire's burning, campfire's burning.
Draw nearer, draw nearer.
In the gloaming, in the gloaming,
Come sing and be merry.

Each Campfire Lights Anew

As your campfire starts to fade out, slowly sing this song to wind down. If you're feeling sad that the experience is over, remind yourself that you'll "come again some other day" and have another fantastic campfire.

Each campfire lights anew
The flame of friendship true.
The joy we've had in knowing you
Will last our whole life through.

And as the embers die away,
We wish that we could ever stay.
But since we cannot have our way,
We'll come again some other day.

Linger

Without question, this is absolutely the best song to end your campfire with. It's sad and sweet and hopeful, all at once. Hum the beginning of each line slowly, and really linger over the lyrics to make it more meaningful.

Hm-mm, I want to linger,
Hm-mm, a little longer,
Hm-mm, a little longer here with you.

Hm-mm, it's such a perfect night,
Hm-mm, it doesn't seem quite right,
Hm-mm, that this should be my last with you.

Hm-mm, and come September,
Hm-mm, I will remember,
Hm-mm, our camping days and friendships
    true.

Hm-mm, and as the years go by,
Hm-mm, I'll think of you and sigh.
Hm-mm, this is goodnight and not goodbye.

Storytelling

A campfire is the ultimate place to tell a spine-tingling ghost story. Most of us live in towns or cities, and are so used to living near other people that we find being out in the peaceful quiet of the woods a little creepy. Darkness surrounds you, with only the flickering glow of the campfire to light the fire circle. Animals you're not used to hearing make strange noises out in the night. And the only people nearby are the ones whose faces you can see by the firelight—you think. This all sets the stage for a chilling round of storytelling.

When you're telling a story, speak with confidence. Don't try to memorize the story exactly, but tell it in your own words. Keep your story fairly short—you don't want your listeners to get bored halfway through. Many storytellers tell the story as if it happened to someone they know, which makes it seem more real.

Use your voice to add to the suspense. Raise your voice and talk faster when someone is being chased in the story, or whisper slowly when a mournful ghost is telling his tale of woe. Give your listeners an extra scare by speaking very softly and then suddenly shouting the last line. Use your movements in the same way. If your story has a sudden reveal that's supposed to make your listeners jump, use your hands to startle them when you shout.

On the pages that follow, you'll find plenty of chills and thrills to fill your next campfire. Some of these stories are classics told at campfires all around the world, while others may be less familiar. Whichever you choose to share, have fun creeping out your friends.

I've Got You Where I Want You

A few years back, there was an old, gloomy gray house that everyone knew was haunted. No one had lived there for many years, and the cobwebs covered the front door. One night, three friends were walking by the house and talking about how creepy it was when one of the kids, a guy named James, dared his friends Lucy and Hector to spend the night in the house's upstairs bedroom.

Lucy just rolled her eyes, but Hector couldn't back down. He agreed to do it.

Hector slowly walked up to the front porch and climbed the steps. Wiping the cobwebs away from the door, he turned the doorknob and cringed at the squealing of the door as it opened. Walking inside, he looked around and sneezed at the dust. "This place sure is dirty, but it's not that bad otherwise," he said to himself. Climbing the stairs, he found the main bedroom and sat on a chair, which creaked under his weight. Humming to himself, he prepared to wait all night for nothing to happen.

Suddenly, a voice cried out, "I've got you where I want you...and now I'm gonna eat you!"

Hector freaked out. A ghost was watching him and was about to turn him into dinner. He burst out of the room and ran down the street.

Seeing Hector run past them, Lucy and James shrugged. James laughed and bragged to Lucy that he could stay in the bedroom longer than Hector had. So he walked up the front porch steps and into the house.

He had barely stepped into the room when he heard the voice.

"I've got you where I want you...and now I'm gonna eat you!"

James turned and ran all the way home, where he didn't come out of his room for a week.

Lucy was really curious now. She knew she should just walk

away, but she just had to find out what had terrified her two friends so. Climbing the stairs to the ancient bedroom, she inhaled deeply. As she entered the room, she didn't see anything unusual. She brushed a thick layer of dust off the bed and sat down. Suddenly, she heard it. A voice, low and rasping.

"I've got you where I want you...and now I'm gonna eat you!"

Lucy was petrified, but she wanted to find out where the voice was coming from. So she listened again.

"I've got you where I want you...and now I'm gonna eat you!"

It sounded like it was coming from the closet across the room. She slowly walked toward the closet as the voice grew louder and more insistent.

"I've got you where I want you...and now I'm gonna eat you!"

She was really getting scared now, but something drew her toward the closet.

"I've got you where I want you...and now I'm gonna eat you!"

She was almost there now. Just a few steps further.

"I've got you where I want you...and now I'm gonna eat you!"

She had her hand on the doorknob now. It was now or never.

"I've got you where I want you...and now I'm gonna eat you!"

She tore open the door and saw...

...a monkey holding a half-eaten banana.

The Bloody Finger

On a dark, gloomy night, a man, his wife, and his three kids were driving down a deserted highway, looking for a place to stay. Suddenly, his wife spotted a dirty, rundown motel with a sign that said "Vacancy". The man pulled into the parking lot and the family piled out of the car. They entered the motel office, but it was deserted. The children looked around, and the son, who was about twelve years old, noticed a bell on the front desk. He rang the bell and its "ding, ding, ding" echoed loudly through the room. Finally, an old man hobbled slowly up to the front desk and said, "Welcome to the Gates Motel."

As the teenage daughter looked around the room in disgust, her father explained to the desk clerk that they had been driving all day long and needed a place to spend the night. The desk clerk looked at the family and shook his head. "Well, I reckon y'all do look mighty tired, but I'm afraid we don't have a vacancy."

The mother, who was holding her four-year-old daughter, looked up in surprise. "But your sign says..."

"That sign's been broken for years," the clerk interrupted. "I wish I had room for y'all, but we only have one double left, and you wouldn't want to stay in it anyway."

"Sir, if you have a room, we'll take it. The kids can sleep on the bed, and my wife and I can sleep in chairs or on the floor, if we have to. We haven't seen another hotel for miles, and we've got to rest," the father said.

The desk clerk looked uncertain. "Well, now...I'm not sure you know what you're getting yourself into, mister. Room 203 is haunted. Every person who's tried to stay in that room for the past twenty years has taken off in the middle of the night, yellin' and hollerin' like the devil was after him. Why, it happens so often, I'd have to ask you to pay the bill up front, in case you aren't around in the morning."

The two parents exchanged amused glances. They clearly thought the desk clerk was a little loopy. "No problem. Here's the money for the room. We'll take it." So, the family went to their car to get their bags, and then climbed up the stairs to room 203. The desk clerk watched them from the lobby, shaking his head.

As the father unlocked the door and slowly opened it, his son suddenly shouted, "Boo!" When his older sister jumped, he laughed. "I got you! I got you!" he said with glee.

She rolled her eyes and walked into the room, followed by the rest of the family. They looked around at the dusty, shabby room. It seemed as if no one had entered the room in at least five years, judging from the amount of dust on the nightstand. But the television still worked, and the kids soon settled down on the bed to watch cartoons while their parents unpacked their overnight bags and got ready for bed.

"Honey, can you please watch the kids for a while," the mother asked her husband. "I'm going to take a warm bath so I can fall asleep quicker."

"Of course, dear. Take your time," he answered, already examining the roadmap to plan his driving route for the next day.

So the mother brought her nightgown into the bathroom and closed the door. She turned on the faucet and let the water run into the tub. But before she could get in and start enjoying her bath, she heard a creepy voice that sounded like it was coming from right behind her. "Oooooooooooooohhhhhhhh...my blooooooooody fiiiiiiiinger!" She looked around, but saw nothing. Scared out of her wits, she ran to the window, jumped out of it,

The Girls' Guide to Campfire Activities

and ran off into the night, screaming.

After a while, the husband looked up from his roadmap and realized his wife had been in the bathroom for a long time. "She probably fell asleep in the tub," he thought to himself. So he knocked on the door and let himself in, closing the door behind him. But when he was in the bathroom, he looked around and didn't see any sign of his wife. Suddenly, he heard the horrible wail, "Ooooooooooooohhhhhhhh...my bloooooooody fiiiiiiiinger!" Terrified he ran to the window, jumped out of it, and ran off into the night, screaming.

A few minutes later, the teenage daughter realized that she really had to pee. So she knocked on the bathroom door, but no one answered. "Hmm, maybe Mom and Dad left to get something out of the car, and we just didn't notice." She opened the bathroom door and went inside. After she used the toilet, she turned the water on in the sink to wash her hands. But suddenly, she heard the scary voice just over her shoulder. "Ooooooooooooohhhhhhhh...my bloooooooody fiiiiiiiinger!" A chill ran down her spine. She ran to the window, jumped out of it, and ran off into the night, screaming.

Meanwhile, the son was hoping to scare his older sister again. So he tiptoed over to the bathroom and listened at the door. When he heard the water running in the sink, he figured it was safe to surprise her, so he quietly opened the door and snuck inside. But when he looked around, he didn't see his sister. Instead, he heard a ghostly voice scream, "Oooooooooooohhhhhhhh...my blooooooody fiiiiiiinger!" Now he jumped with fear. Inside he knew that voice was a mournful soul, and not his sister playing a joke back on him. So he ran to the window, jumped out of it, and ran off into the night, screaming.

When the cartoon show was over, the younger sister

decided she was thirsty. She slid off the bed and carried her plastic cup over to the bathroom. The door was slightly ajar, so she pushed it open and walked into the room. She couldn't quite reach the sink, so she turned over the trash can and used it as a step stool. The water was still running, so she reached her cup under its steady stream. Just then, she heard a voice. "Ooooooooooooohhhhhhhh...my blooooooody fiiiiiiinger!" She looked around, but didn't see anything. But she was used to creepy voices, since her brother was always teasing their older sister with them.

Then, she heard it wail again, louder this time. "Ooooooooooooohhhhhhhh...my blooooooody fiiiiiiinger!" She wasn't so sure it was her brother after all.

Suddenly, the voice screamed once more, right over her shoulder. "OOOOOOOOOOOOOHHHHHHHH...MY BLOOOOOOODY FIIIIIIINGER!"

So the little girl answered, "Then put a Band Aid on it!" And she hopped down off the trash can, went back to the other room, and watched cartoons until she fell asleep.

J.J.'s Ghost

Many years ago, a mean old man lived in a big, white farmhouse. He had once been a successful farmer, until a horrible accident damaged his leg and gave him a heavy limp. Now, he rarely left the house and kept his beautiful daughter, Sarah, locked up with him.

The only time Sarah was allowed to leave the house without her father was on Sundays when she went to church. It was there that she met J.J., a handsome young man who happened to live on a neighboring farm. Unfortunately, Sarah's father and J.J.'s family were enemies who'd had many arguments and property

 disputes during the years.

Sarah knew that her father would never allow her to marry J.J., so they planned to elope one evening. The only problem was that her father always locked her in her room at night before he went to bed.

So the two young lovers planned her escape—she would crawl down the tree outside her bedroom window.

The night of the elopement came, and Sarah's father locked her in the room as usual. Sarah packed her things and waited for J.J.'s arrival. At midnight, she heard J.J. whisper her name outside. But just then, she heard her father walking down the hall, dragging his bad leg behind him. Slide, THUMP. Slide, THUMP. Slide, THUMP.

Her heart was beating fast. She knew that her father would rather kill J.J. than let him marry his only daughter. She threw her suitcase down to J.J. as her father drew closer and started moving faster. Slide, THUMP. Slide, THUMP. Slide, THUMP.

Sarah was really getting anxious now, because her father was right outside her door. She quickly crawled out the window and out onto the tree branch. J.J. called out to her, "Hurry, Sarah. But be careful." A key rattled in the lock, and the door slowly creaked open. Through the open window, Sarah could hear her father galloping across the room. Slide, THUMP. Slide, THUMP. Slide, THUMP.

Sarah kept glancing up at the window while she climbed down the tree, looking for her father and his shotgun. Suddenly, she saw her father in the window. As she shivered in fear at the hatred on his face, she reached out for the next branch, but missed it, falling to her death. J.J. cried out in pain and kneeled down to embrace Sarah's lifeless body.

Meanwhile, Sarah's father was furious at J.J. for stealing his precious daughter away from him. Blinded by rage, he slowly pulled his shotgun up and set it on the window ledge. Slide, THUMP. He took aim at his enemy and fired. J.J. didn't even flinch. If he couldn't be with his beloved in life, at least he could join her in death.

But Sarah's father had one more plan to keep the young lovers apart. Instead of burying Sarah in the local cemetery, where she would be close to J.J., he placed her body in a separate gravesite on the opposite hillside.

Locals swear that on nights like this one, just as the bell tolls midnight, you can see J.J.'s ghost wandering that hillside, trying in vain to find his beloved Sarah.

The Hitchhiker

One dark, rainy night, a young man was driving home from the homecoming dance. It was very late and he was having trouble seeing the road when his headlights suddenly picked up a large white object on the side of the road. He slowed down and saw that this object was, in fact, a young woman in a white dress, soaked to the bone.

Pulling over, the young man offered to give the woman a ride home, which she gladly accepted. He'd never seen her before, but thought she was very beautiful. He thought it was a little strange that she was walking home in the rain, but guessed that she'd gotten separated from her friends at the dance and tried to walk home by herself.

As he watched her, he noticed she was shivering. So, being a nice guy, he offered her his varsity letter jacket to wear.

As she warmed up, they talked all the way home. The young man really began to like his beautiful hitchhiker, and decided to ask her out when he dropped her off. All too soon they arrived at her house, and he got out to open her door. But when he got to the other side of the car, the passenger door was already open, and she was gone.

"That's a little weird," he thought, but figured she'd run into the house while he was walking around the car.

The next morning, the young man couldn't find his letter jacket. Suddenly, he remembered—the young woman hadn't taken it off before she went inside. So, he drove back to her house, glad to have an excuse to talk to her again. He walked up to the front porch and rang the doorbell. Soon, a woman answered. Figuring that the woman was his hitchhiker's mother, he explained that he'd given her daughter a ride home the previous night, and that she'd forgotten to give him back his jacket.

The woman looked at him in anger. "Is this some kind of a joke?" she asked.

"No, I'm sorry if I'm getting her into trouble, but she really needed a ride home," he tried to explain.

But the woman shook her head and said, "My daughter died in a car accident nearly ten years ago. So there's no way she could have been in the car with you last night."

The young man was horrified. He couldn't believe what she was telling him. It just couldn't be true.

The woman told him where her daughter had been buried so that the young man could see for himself. As he pulled up to the cemetery, he knew immediately which grave was hers, for hanging on the tombstone was his varsity letter jacket.

Good Night Games

Things look very different during the night than they do during the day. Take a break from your campfire (leaving someone to keep an eye on it, of course) to do one of these nighttime–only activities.

Stargaze

The area around your campsite is probably a lot darker than the neighborhood where you live. That's why you can see more stars when you're in rural areas, away from the light pollution of cities and towns. Take advantage of this viewing opportunity by looking up at the night sky while you're sitting around the campfire. Before you go, look for stargazing information on the Internet or read a book about constellations so that you know what you're looking at.

Take a Night Hike

A night hike is the perfect time to exercise your senses. The night may seem pitch black at first, but as your eyes adjust you'll be surprised by how many things you can see. To stay safe, you and your friends should walk in a line with your hands on the shoulders of the person in front of you. The leader should bring a flashlight in case it's needed. Walk slowly to find your footing and don't speak or make noise. The best part of this hike is just listening to the peaceful world around you.

Sounds Like Night

See how many different sounds you can hear in the darkness. Walk a short distance from your campsite with a paper and pencil and find a good place to sit down. Silently listen to everything around you and make a map of where different sounds came from. Try to identify what kind of animal or natural element made the sound. When you return to your campfire, compare notes with your friends and see who has the best ears.

CHAPTER 3

How to Host a Campfire in Your Very Own Living Room

Can't convince your friends to rough it for a weekend of camping fun, but still want that special campfire experience? No worries! With a little creativity you can pack all of the fire, food, and fun of a campfire into your own cozy living room.

Pre-Party Planning

Before the big night, you'll want to do some planning.
Here's a little checklist to help you get organized.

- ❏ Make and send invitations with a camping theme.
- ❏ Decide what snacks you'll want to make and write a shopping list.
- ❏ Choose a type of indoor campfire and collect any materials that you'll need.
- ❏ Buy or make party favors.
- ❏ Decorate the room.
- ❏ Choose a couple of camp-themed movies to watch and rent them.
- ❏ Find a CD or songbook with camp songs to sing.
- ❏ Learn a couple of ghost stories.

It's All about the Invite

Tell your friends about your cool campfire party by giving them homemade invites. Use construction paper to make one of these fun invitations or create your own.

- ☉ A s'more
- ☉ A sleeping bag that flips open to show the details
- ☉ A snack-sized plastic bag that contains two small graham cookies, a mini chocolate bar, and a few mini marshmallows, along with a sticker giving the time and place.
- ☉ A campfire with yellow flames for writing on
- ☉ Cards with photos of your favorite wild animals
- ☉ A tent with flaps that open to reveal the information

Decoration Station

Make your guests feel like they're in the outdoors by decorating your room with nature-themed items. Hide some wild stuffed animals in their "natural" habitats—monkeys hanging from the bookshelves, raccoons scooting under a table, bears on the chairs. Find a nature sounds CD and play it softly as your guests arrive so that they can hear the bullfrogs welcoming the dark. Bring extra plants into your room to give it more of a forest feel. Ask an adult if you can put glow-in-the-dark star stickers on the ceiling to make constellations (push them on gently if you need to take them off later).

Bringing the Fire Indoors

When you're hosting an indoor campfire, you'll definitely need some kind of fire to sit around. But it doesn't have to be real flames—an onscreen fire or fake fire will work just as well. Before you "light" your fire, set the mood by turning off all or most of the lights.

Must-See TV

For the best in high-tech fire building, simply pop the disc that came with this book into your DVD player and press play. Before you know it, you'll have a roaring campfire on your television screen, complete with sound effects. You won't want to sit there watching it for hours, but it does help to set the mood while you make your snacks, sing

sings, and tell stories. There's no worry about putting out the fire, either—just eject the DVD and put it back in this book for safekeeping.

Tissue Paper Fire

If you and your friends want a 3-D campfire that's safe to sleep around, try making this bright and cheerful fake fire. But don't light it or get it close to open flame—it's just for looks.

YOU'LL NEED:

- A small tablecloth
- 9 clean logs, about $1\frac{1}{2}$ inches in diameter
- Yellow, orange, and red tissue paper

1. Fold the tablecloth into a circle or square about 16 inches across. Place it in the middle of your space.
2. Put three logs on the tablecloth, overlapping them in a triangle shape.
3. Stack three more logs on top of the triangle, overlapping them more to make a smaller triangle. Repeat with the last three logs.
4. Tear the tissue paper into squares about 1 foot by 1 foot.
5. Find the middle point of each square and put your pointer finger on it. Using your other

hand, squeeze the tissue paper up around your finger so the paper looks like a closed umbrella. Remove your finger.

6. Stick the tips of the tissue paper squares into the log pyramid to make flames. Remember that a fire burns redder towards its center, and the outermost flames look yellow.

A Real Indoor Fire

On a cold winter's night, there's nothing like curling up in your sleeping bag with a roaring fire in the fireplace. If you're lucky enough to have a working fireplace (and adults who are willing to help you build a fire in it), your indoor campfire will feel authentic—minus the dirt and bugs. Follow these steps to build the perfect indoor fire. You'll find that your outdoor fire-building skills will come in handy.

1. Shovel and throw away any ashes that have been left in the fireplace. With an adult's help, check to make sure that the chimney damper is open.

2. Bring an armful of fuel (hardwood logs work well) to the fireplace. Also collect a large handful of kindling

(smaller softwood pieces such as pine) and some tinder (newspaper).

3. Twist or crumple four or five sheets of newspaper and place them on your fire grate. Building a fire on a grate allows air to feed the fire.

4. Gently set kindling pieces over the tinder, being careful to leave some space below them.

5. With an adult's help, use a match to light the tinder in several places.

6. Once the tinder has set fire to the kindling, place two or three small pieces of fuel on top of the kindling.

7. As the fuel begins to burn, add another piece of fuel occasionally to keep the fire going strong.

8. To put out the fire, stop adding fuel and let it die down. Use fire tongs to carefully spread the coals so they cool off. Allow the ashes to cool completely before removing them. As with a campfire, check the ashes by holding your hand a foot above them. If you do not feel any heat, slowly lower your hand until you feel heat or are within an inch of the ashes.

9. Once the fire is out, close the damper to keep warm air inside the house.

Keep the Fire in the Fireplace

Houses, and the furniture inside them, are often built from flammable materials. Keep the fire where it belongs by following these safety rules.

1. Move all flammable objects, such as rugs, toys, magazines, and decorations, away from the fireplace before starting a fire.

2. Check to make sure the damper is open before you start the fire. The damper allows smoke to rise up through the chimney, not out into your room.

3. Always use a fire screen or metal curtain on your fireplace. Keep it tightly closed when you are not working on the fire so sparks are kept inside the fireplace.

4. Use metal fire tools to tend the fire.

5. Roasting marshmallows over a fireplace fire is not recommended because they could catch on fire and spread it to the house. Also, the fireplace doesn't allow much room for movement and the marshmallows usually make a big mess. Try one of our alternative methods instead.

Fun Party Foods

If you're craving campfire-roasted marshmallows and messy s'mores but you're stuck inside, try these yummy substitutes. They have all the sweet taste sensation without the mess—and without that smoky campfire smell!

Mini Marshmallow Roast

If you don't have a working fireplace, here's a safe and simple way to get the fun of roasting marshmallows without creating a big mess. Use fondue forks instead of toothpicks if you have them. Makes as many mini marshmallows as you can eat.

YOU'LL NEED:

- Wooden toothpicks
- Tealight candles
- Matches
- Mini marshmallows

DO THIS:

1. Soak the toothpicks in water for 30 minutes. Drain.
2. With an adult's help, light a tealight candle for each person.
3. Put a mini marshmallow on a toothpick and roast it over your candle, about an inch above the flame. Try not to catch it on fire, but blow it out quickly if it does.
4. Enjoy!

Indoor S'mores

This no-mess indoor version of the classic s'mores may not be as much fun as roasting marshmallows on a stick, but it's a lot faster. This recipe calls for less chocolate and marshmallow than our Ooey Gooey S'mores because the oven melts the chocolate more, giving it plenty of chocolaty goodness. Makes 8 s'mores.

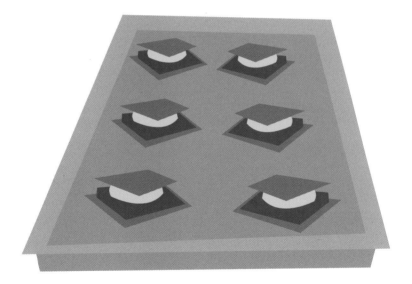

YOU'LL NEED:

- 8 graham crackers
- 2 milk chocolate bars, such as Hershey's
- Aluminum foil
- 8 marshmallows

1. Line a baking pan with foil. With an adult's help, preheat your oven or toaster oven to broil.
2. Carefully break each graham cracker in half to make two squares. Place them in a single layer on the foil.
3. Break each chocolate bar into four pieces (each containing three little rectangles). Place each chocolate piece on a graham cracker half.
4. Place one marshmallow on each of the remaining eight graham cracker squares.
5. Carefully put the pan into the oven and broil for about 1 minute, or until the marshmallows are just turning golden brown.
6. Remove the pan from the oven and fold the two halves of each s'more together. Serve immediately.

Mini Microwave S'mores

These super-cute bite-size s'mores only take minutes to make, and they taste like the real thing. Make a bunch to share with your friends! Makes 8 mini s'mores.

YOU'LL NEED:

- 16 small graham-flavored cookies, such as Teddy Grahams
- 16 milk chocolate chips
- 8 mini marshmallows

1. Place the cookies face down on a microwave-safe plate.
2. Carefully put two chocolate chips each on half of the cookies.
3. Add a mini marshmallow to each of the remaining cookies.
4. Microwave the cookies for about 30 seconds. (Some microwaves are stronger than others, so adjust the time as necessary.)
5. Take one chocolate-covered cookie and one marshmallow-covered cookie and squeeze them together to make a s'more. Repeat with the remaining cookies. Serve immediately.

Fondue S'mores

When you crave your campfire favorites but want a sophisticated edge, try this twist on the old favorite. Make a big batch of chocolate fondue and sit around the pot dipping marshmallows into it with your friends. Makes 4 to 6 servings.

YOU'LL NEED:

- 10 graham crackers
- 1 bag of milk chocolate chips (11½ ounces)
- ⅓ cup milk
- 1 bag of marshmallows
- Fondue forks or regular forks

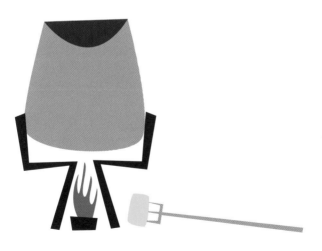

1. Using a food processor, grind five graham crackers into crumbs. (Or, put them into a sealed plastic bag and crush them into crumbs with a wooden spoon.) Pour into a bowl with deep sides and repeat with the remaining five graham crackers. Set aside.

2. Pour the chocolate chips and the milk into a heavy $1^1/_2$-quart saucepan.

3. With an adult's help, heat the saucepan over low heat, stirring constantly. When the chocolate has melted and the milk has disappeared, pour the mixture into a bowl.

4. To eat the fondue, put a marshmallow on a fondue fork. Dip it into the chocolate and then hold it over the bowl for a few seconds to drip, then roll the marshmallow in the graham cracker crumbs. Enjoy and repeat.

5. If the chocolate cools down or thickens too much, reheat it in the microwave at 50% power for 1 minute to warm up. Stir and continue dipping.

Late-Night Stuff

After you've snacked sing a few songs and tell some ghost stories. If you're still wide awake once you've put your "campfire" out, play a game or put a camp-themed movie in the DVD player. Or, just have some girl talk in the dark until you all fall asleep in the wee hours.

Pitch Dark Art

Have fun in the dark by drawing pictures when you can't see. Then, turn on the lights and admire your art—or laugh at the ridiculous results!

YOU'LL NEED:

- Paper
- Markers
- Things to write on (like books or clipboards)

1. Give each person a piece of paper, a marker, and something hard to write on.
2. Turn off all the lights. If you can't get the room completely dark, ask everyone to close their eyes.
3. Think of something for everyone to draw and tell them what it is. Tell them to start and count to 20 silently.
4. When the time is up, turn on the lights. Compare pictures and vote for the best picture. The winner chooses the theme for the next turn.

Flashlight Tag

What do you get when you combine the popular games of tag and hide-and-seek? This great slumber party game! You can play it inside or out, as long as you have a large, dark area that doesn't have too many obstacles on the ground (like toys or tree stumps) to trip you up. Just put on your darkest clothes, and go hide!

YOU'LL NEED:

- A dark room or backyard
- A flashlight

1. Agree on the boundaries of the play area and a jail. Pick a person to be "It". She sits at the jail and counts to twenty while everyone else runs and hides.

2. Once "It" has finished counting to twenty, she turns on her flashlight and tries to find the people who are hiding. She must always keep her flashlight on and uncovered. The hiders can change hiding places during the game, but must always stay inbounds.

3. When "It" finds someone, she "tags" the person by shining the flashlight on her and calling out the person's name. If she is correct, the person must go to jail. If not, the person can hide again.

4. Once all of the people hiding have been sent to jail, the first person who was tagged during that game is the new "It".

Variations

- For a shorter game, end the game when the first person is caught and have everyone else come out of hiding. The first person caught becomes "It" and starts a new game.

- For a large group, make several people "It". While

this team of people is trying to catch people who are hiding, the hiders can rescue people who have already been caught and sent to jail by sneaking up to the jail and tagging the "prisoners" with their hands. However, a member of the "It" team can stay near the jail to guard it.

Great Camping Movies

When you're ready to settle in for a movie, pop in one of these great camping flicks and pretend like you're in the great outdoors.

- *Addams Family Values* (1993, PG-13) While Uncle Fester deals with a new girlfriend, Wednesday drives her camp counselors crazy.
- *Camp* (2003, PG-13) Teens strive to be the best at a performing arts summer camp.
- *Camp Nowhere* (1994, PG) A group of friends create the best camp in the world—a fake one.
- *Ernest Goes to Camp* (1987, PG) A maintenance man becomes a camp counselor for juvenile delinquents in this comedy.

- *The Great Outdoors* (1988, PG) A family's lake vacation is interrupted by the arrival of their obnoxious relatives.
- *Heavyweights* (1995, PG) Kids at a fat camp rebel against the new owner, played by Ben Stiller.
- *Meatballs* (1979, PG) This comedy stars Bill Murray as a wacky camp counselor at a sleepaway camp.
- *The Parent Trap* (1961, G) Separated as babies, twins find each other at camp and hatch a plan to bring their parents back together.
- *The Parent Trap* (1998, PG) This remake of the 1961 classic stars Lindsay Lohan in dual roles.
- *Troop Beverly Hills* (1989, PG) A scout troop from Beverly Hills does things their own way in this comedy.
- *Without a Paddle* (2004, PG-13) A canoe trip through the wilderness goes hilariously wrong for three young men.

Do Me a Favor

Send your friends home with a useful reminder of their night around the campfire. These camp–themed party favors are sure to be favorites, or come up with your own ideas.

- Mini flashlights
- A pocket guide to the constellations
- Colorful bandanas
- A small backpack
- A book about ghost stories

ELIZABETH ENCARNACION has been a Girl Scout for twenty-seven years, and is a current Girl Scout leader who takes her city-based troop on yearly camping trips. She has camped, built fires, cooked s'mores, sung camp songs, and told scary ghost stories all across North America, from the Appalachian Trail to the Grand Tetons, and from the Canadian Quetico to the Florida Keys. When she's not roughing it in the outdoors, she writes and edits books for kids and teens, including the *Fabulous Fun Foam Book & Kit*, a novelization of the *Rudolph the Red-Nosed Reindeer* television special, and the four-book *Buildings at Work* series. Visit her on the Web at www.elizabethencarnacion.com.

About Applesauce Press

What kid doesn't love Applesauce!

Applesauce Press was created to press out the best children's books found anywhere. Like our parent company, Cider Mill Press Book Publishers, we strive to bring fine reading, information, and entertainment to kids of all ages. Between the covers of our creatively crafted books, you'll find beautiful designs, creative formats, and most of all, kid-friendly information on pressing [important] topics. Our Cider Mill bears fruit twice a year, publishing a new crop of titles each spring and fall.